That Cowherd Boy of VRINDAVAN

Written By
Shruti Ray

In the memory of my Spiritual Master

HG MADHUSUDHAN MAHARAJ

Published By

True Dreamster Press

ISBN: 978-93-6288-282-0
MRP: Rs.229/-

Printed in India

ABOUT THE BOOK

This book takes you on a journey of knowing Krishna, the divine boy of Vrindavan. It has poems and short stories inspired by the tales told by devotees and residents of Vrindavan. The book gives you the perspective of a devotee, of you being introduced to him by his devotees, at first you get intrigued, and eventually, you are left enchanted by the divine boy just like them.

CONTENTS

THAT COWHERD BOY OF VRINDAVAN

INTRODUCTION

Have you ever heard about him? You must have, some would say he is a naughty child who steals butter from their *matkas*, some would say he is the mighty lord who saved them from *Asuras*.

For mothers he is a baby playing in their lap, for Gopis he is a lover stealing their hearts.
For Gopas he is a mischievous friend, for others he is the lord.
He is so merciful, he plays any role, the devotee wants.

One Glimpse

They warned me enough, to know
If you are to be captivated
Just one glimpse of him, can do so

Be as careful as you can be
As once you get entangled in his charms
There is no way to become free

You stumble upon his beauty
And your eyes get stuck
Overwhelmed by his glory
You are left awestruck

Monsoon cloud hue, the color of his body
Yellow garments wrapped around it
A turban adorned with peacock feathers
And nectar flowing from his lotus feet

Up and down, your eyes keep moving
But they can't look away
You notice his wide eyes and then him smiling
You never knew what was coming your way

It happens faster than you realize
Before you know what to do
You are already drowning in his wide eyes
I am telling you just the way they told me to
Be careful
If you are to be captivated
His one glimpse will do

Where should I begin?

You asked me to describe him
Where should I begin?
Should I tell you about his sweet nature?
Or his sweet face

Should I describe, his naughty behavior
Or his greatness
Should I tell you about his infinite mercy?
Or about how protective he is about his devotees

Do you want to know about
The unlimited love he gives
Or how he gets happy like a child
When you are giving your love and he receives

I can tell you all I want
But how much can I tell?
After all he is the supreme almighty lord
And I am just a cowherd girl under his spell.

So wonderful!

Oh, what's so wonderful about him? You ask
I say he is full of wonders,
Finding one would be a task
Oh just look at him

How can somebody be?
So composed and playful simultaneously
He is a child playing with mud yet the master of the universe
If you are good, he is better, if you are bad he is worse

Oh, he is naughty yet so lovable
He is so great yet so humble
He is a friend, a son, a lover
He becomes all yours even when, for the world he is the only master
He is so wonderful!

Dilemma

Call him an illusionist or call him a black magician!
One thought that I am certain of
That he loves to put us in confusion

He will pull all kind of tricks on you
And even though you want to scold him
You won't be able to

He will put you through a dilemma
You won't be able to decide, whether to complain or praise?
Such is his charisma

Teasing you all he wants
Pulling your hair and breaking your pot
But even if you pretend, that you want him to stop
You somehow end up, cherishing his taunts

They warn you to stay away from him
You warn yourself too
Yet your eyes keep searching
You say you don't want to see him, but is that true?

O Butter

The Gopis put you in pots, not letting a drop go to waste
Then hang it high safely, until someone gets your taste

There you wait hanging
And then you hear someone whispering
Behind the close doors
The naughty son of Yashoda, telling to his friends
"Be quick the Gopi will return from her chores"

He then enters silently
And climb the back of his mate
Holding the pot firmly, he brings you down
What a lovely fate!
You are smeared all over his lips
And from his clothes and fingers, you drip

He eats you a bit and then share with his friend
Laughing and joking, the bliss
Doesn't seem to end
Until the Gopi arrives
And him and his Sakhas
Run for their lives

O butter, your fortune, is beyond belief
To get you, the lord himself has become a thief

That Morning at the Bank of Yamuna

The sun painted the horizon crimson red
The birds woke up from slumber
Gopis strolled on the path that led
Towards the banks of the river,

The hushed sound of their footsteps
As they walked the path ahead
Stopped when they heard
The sound of flute approaching them

They stood as if the time paused too
With closed eyes and lips stretched in a smile
All they could hear was the flute
It was only after a while

They realized,
The music couldn't be heard anymore
They came to their senses but got lost again
When they saw that beautiful boy standing before

The river rushed at his lotus feet
The branches swayed with his peacock feather
The flute drinking the nectar of his lips- Oh so sweet!
The Gopis kept drowning in his aura, as the sun rose higher

Lover of devotees

Krishna's love for his devotees is pure and unconditional
Dear friend you don't even know
For him you are so much special

You must think I love him, but I am so faulty
Will he love me back?
Then remember you don't need
To spend a second thought on that

He loves you like nobody else can
He cherishes you like bee cherishes nectar
He preserves you like one preserves rare treasure
You might have faults but all the good hidden within
Is seen by him

Nothing can escape those Kamal Nayan

Instead of this beautiful world
He created
His favorite view is
You looking at him

Just like he is your universe
His world revolves around you
Just like you fall for him
He falls for you too

He smiles when you smile
He feels the pain of your hurt
He readily walks miles

When you take a step forward

Even though you may not understand his love for you
To him, you are precious and always be
His love for you will never change
Assures he

Although he owns the three worlds
He says proudly
- 'I am not free, I belong to my devotees'

Playing in the waters

As the water glistened in the broad noon
He and his Sakhas arrived at the Kund
They jumped in straight to cool off the heat

They splashed and plunged in and out
The banks echoing with their shouts
Enjoying their past times tirelessly,
Not even pausing to breathe

While he plays, he gets wet from head to toe
Bouncing, diving, pulling and pushing
Look at them moving
So gracefully, as if putting a show

Simple games bring endless joys
Krishna's presence is so precious to
These cowherd boys
Even the animals jump in to play with them
Even the creepers entangle his lotus feet
As if they
Are joining his play.

You Are My Home

Dear Krishna
For some you are a friend
For some you are a mentor
For some you are savior
For some a lover
For a poet you are inspiration
You are muse for artists
You are the only subject of love for devotees
But you are 'home' to me

You are someone in front of whom I can cry freely
For I won't be judged but helped
Where being afraid is not so scary
Because you will protect
Where I can be silly
As I know you are always there
And I love it the most how you don't care

That I am ugly or pretty
If I am stupid or smarty
All you care about is that I am yours, and how you claim it so proudly
And what amazes me the most
That after whatever I did or do
You still became mine, so readily
O Krishna, you are my home,
You are the only shelter I desire desperately

Cowherd Boy

I Fell in love with a cowherd boy
Now I am drowning in his eyes
Do you think I will die?
Oh, look at how he smiles like he
Knows what he did but still denies
Do you think does it purposely?
Steal our heart from us and then smile widely

Isn't he the all merciful lord
Shouldn't he show us some mercy
Still he robs us poor girls
Steal our life then mock us
Says he didn't do anything
But then how do you explain
That you became our everything!

Now all that I see is blue
Now all that I hear is the flute
Now all that I can think of is
You

Now at Every corner of the street
My keen eyes wait innocently
Just to take a quick peek
And when it gets a quick glance
I know how you smirk at our naivety

I know even though
You don't show
You enjoy it somewhere within

Playing with our hearts so casually

You say you didn't
But I am sure you did something
Even when you claim you are innocent
We know it's your doing

No questions please

They ask 'when'
I say I don't remember
They ask how
And I don't have any answer

They warned me yes they did say
From that little blue boy, "stay away"

Don't ask me again and again, because I don't know
How he stole my heart, even before I could say 'No'

But why him? You ask again
And yet I find it hard to explain

How can I make you believe me?
Have you ever seen someone stealing so innocently?
You try to understand but you don't
And you won't
Until one day you yourself drown in those wide eyes
The magic that smile casts upon you will suffice
He will steal you from you
And there would be nothing left to say nor anything that you could do

In the meadows

Tired from running around
Gopal decided to take rest and sat down
While caressing his little calf, he slowly took out his flute
And touched it with his lips- whose redness resembled the bimba fruit
He breathed life into it, holding it in his lotus hands
The music spread all over the grasslands
The cows stopped eating
The Gopas stopped playing
The music enchanted every living being
But for the Gopis, the music did something more
They stood lifeless abandoning their ongoing chores
Their body shivering, their eyes teary but lip smiling

Look at shri Radhika the queen of Vrindavan
Hearing the flute playing, she is eagerly searching for her Madanmohan
The brajwasis have lost themselves in you
Oh Krishna what did you do?

Oh to be!

Oh to be someone
Who can tell your glories to the world
I dream to be a writer who can find the right words
The words that can justify
Words that can suffice
Words that would actually carry that aura, show them where my heart resides

Oh to be
Someone who can sing your glories
I dream to be a singer who can find the right notes and melodies
That can take them in my heart
Make them feel what I feel
When you enchant me

Oh to be
Someone who can bring your image to life
Make it tangible what she sees in her mind
Oh, I dream to be
A painter that can fill the canvas just like her memory
To be able to show them your unexplainable beauty

Oh to be an artist,
An artist who is skilled enough
To show the within
To make them feel the trance we are put in

But alas!
No can do

Because in front of you
a writer is in loss for words
a singer can't find the right note
and a painter will never be satisfied with her own work

They will never be able to find the skill that is able to
actually, in wholeness tell or show
The world
There will be always more
to add
more of it, within the heart
one will never be able to fully explain or understand
what you are!

Looking at him

Looking at him
Is as living in a daydream
Soothing and relaxing
Just like my face being touched by summer breeze

His beauty so poetic
Like a poet's masterpiece

As I keep looking at him
I am getting addicted to it

It's like listening to
My favorite song on repeat
The feeling hits
Just like that quote, I underlined
In my favorite book
Looking at him
Is the comfort that hugs me
When I smell my favorite food

My eyes watery
My heart at ease
Lips can't stop smiling
My body stuck in constant freeze

As if the time has paused
Here I am at loss of words,
What they say being speechless
Especially when my heart yearns to praise
Your wide eyes with that piercing gaze

That smile that brightens the darkest days
That complexion that resembles
The monsoon clouds in the month of may
I want to say words that describe you
But at the end what can I say

Because I am not able to think
I am sure I had a lot to say
But I forgot everything
That's what happens whenever I am
looking at him

O Radha!

O Radha!
I plead before you
Tell me what should I do

I want to please your Murlidhar
But I don't know how and what to offer?

First, I thought I should offer some flowers- colourful and pretty
Then I thought, you, radharani are prettier than any flower can be
Then maybe I should offer some sweets- some kheer, some jalebis
But then it came to me
You are sweeter than pure jaggery

Then maybe I should offer some jewelries
But then again, you are beautiful and brighter than any Ratna Manis
Hey Barsane Wali
I thought for a long while
And later realized, nothing can please Krishna, more
Than you, your pleasure and your smile

O dear Srimati
Please bestow your mercy upon me
Let me be yours and please your beloved Hari

THE THIEF

It was middle of the day, after finishing all her other chores, Yashoda maiya sat churning butter in her courtyard.

Her lala had become very picky about his food and won't eat anything until maiya gave him fresh butter.

She tried to be strict with him and said he had to eat what was given or go hungry.

Half of the day has already gone and her stubborn Gopal hasn't touched food yet
Even though she wanted to discipline her child, how can she let him stay hungry.

So she sat there churning fresh butter for her son.

She kept thinking about his little hands, his sweet talk, and his childish habits.

"Nandrani! Nandrani" a Gopi came running
"What happened why are you so anxious dear?" Yashoda maiya enquired

"Why don't you ask your son? Aren't you the queen of Nandmaharaj, why your son is going around stealing from us poor Gopis?" She said

Yashoda maiya looked at her with utter confusion she couldn't believe her ears
"What do you mean by it?" Yashoda maiya asked again

"Nandrani I was at my home doing house hold chores, suddenly I heard loud noise of pot cracking, when I reached

over there I saw all my butter scattered on the floor and your lala and his friends escaping from the window"
Yashoda maiya was shocked to hear this
But before she could say anything another Gopi came running in

"Nandrani Nandrani, your Gopal stole my butter," She yelled

Yashoda maiya was even more shocked.
"Yashoda, o Yashoda look what your son has done" came running another two Gopis
But this time they were drenched in butter from head to toe.

"What happened?" Yashoda maiya looked at them with confusion while the other Gopis tried to contain their chuckles

"What else, we were going to the market to sell this butter, your beloved son stopped us mid-way and demanded that we gave our butter to him, when we refused, his friends stopped us from leaving and when we still refused, he broke our pots with stones"

All the Gopis looked at Yashoda with anger
"You punish him or we shall punish your lala on our own"
They said with anger

"Lala!" maiya Yashoda called her son

Krishna came slowly walking in, his clothes disheveled, and he had smudged his mascara as he rubbed his eye.

"What happened, maiya?" he said after taking a long yawn

"Where were you?" maiya asked
"Sleeping" he said in all innocence

"These Gopis have come to complain. Tell me, did you really steal their butter?" Maiya Yashoda asked in a stern voice

"Steal? Me? From them?" Krishna asked in pure confusion

"Maiya, I am the son of Nand Maharaj, if I wanted something, Baba would give it to me without any delay, why would I steal anything?"
He spoke

Gopis became even angrier.
Not only did this beautiful child of Yashoda steal their butter, but he was also cunningly lying and acting in front of his mother
"Don't lie, Krishna!" I saw you with my own eyes. It was you who stole butter from my house
"You must have been mistaken, Gopi", Krishna replied with a smile
The Gopi was flustered. How can she be mistaken
It was surely Krishna himself
That complexion, those beautiful dark hair curls, those tender arms and legs, those beautiful lotus eyes and lips, that majestic peacock feather on his head, there was no way that was someone else other than him.

"Even if I believe she was mistaken, how do you explain our plight, Krishna?" the Gopis drenched in butter said
"Look at us!" She pleaded
"Oh Gopi, you should walk carefully. Even before your mother-in-law has scolded you for being careless and

breaking the pots, you should keep your eyes on the road while walking, and hold your pots firmly. Look what has happened to you," that innocent boy said with concern

The Gopis flustered, didn't know what to say or even think It was true her mother-in-law had caught her many times lost in thoughts and being careless with pots, but it wasn't her fault, who could resist the thoughts of that bewitcher- Krishna.

Even today, she and her friend were busy talking about him, when suddenly he popped up with his friends demanding butter.

And now she stood there, confused about whether it was really him or her imagination.

"Yashoda maiya, your son is great at pretending. I wonder where he learnt the art of lying from", one Gopi said
"O Krishna, you could fool them, but I am sure I saw you take out that butter at my house for sure", She said

"Maiya, even if you want to believe them, how can I be present at all the places, all together, while I was sleeping here in Nand Bhavan, you say I was present at Laxmi's house and Chandra's house, and I even stopped Prabha and Jyoti on the way to the market"

Said the omnipresent lord, as if he is not present in every single being as well as resting on his Sheshnaag in the cosmic ocean.

Yes, he is the same lord, but here he cherishes his role as a cowherd boy in the village of Vrindavan, playing with the naive Gopis.
Nandrani looked at the Gopis and then at her child.
The Gopis had nothing else to say, no word came out of their mouth without fumbling. In this condition, how can they argue with that witty son of Nandmaharaj?
They left quietly.

Krishna looked at his mother hopefully.
She said nothing; she knew the Gopis were not lying.
She was disappointed. She quietly went inside. Krishna understood his mother is upset, and now this made him anxious.
It was already dawn, and Yashoda Maiya still wasn't talking with her dear lala.
"Maiyaa, are you upset with me?" Little Kanha looked at his maiya with pleading eyes.
"Balaram, tell your brother that I do not talk with thieves", Maiya Yashoda said.

Krishna looked at Balaram, who himself felt sorry for his little brother.
Maiya Yashoda kept herself busy with chores while her little boy kept following her around.
He pulled his saree and kept calling her.
"Yashoda, Kanha is still a child, he has apologized too, don't be so harsh on him" Maa Rohini took Kanhaiya's side.
Mother Yashoda, who kept avoiding meeting her child's eyes, finally looked at him.
Looking at those tear filled eyes, she couldn't restrain herself anymore
She picked up her child and hugged him.

"I don't want you to go around stealing from those Gopis again", maiya Yashoda said sternly.
Krishna nodded.

Days went by
The Gopis noticed the little thief's absence.
But they weren't happy as they should have been.
They were missing the beautiful boy running around their houses, his laugh and smart comments when they failed to catch him.

One afternoon, they saw Krishna laughing and talking with his friends.
Jyoti went to him and asked, "O Krishna, what is so funny? Tell us also"
Krishna stayed silent and walked ahead.
"Come, friends, we will go somewhere else, if we stay here for long, they will complain to my mother that I didn't let them complete their work on time"
He said
Gopis were upset on hearing this; all they wanted was to see him again, argue with him a little bit, to engage in those fun banters again. If Krishna wouldn't talk with them again, how would they live?

They went to Nandranı again.
"Yashoda, o Yashoda", all of them went to her with their plea.

"What happened?" Yashoda maiya asked as she came outside. She was wary that her child had done something again.
"Yashoda maiya, what did you tell your child?" one Gopi began complaining

"Why? Did he steal again? I clearly told him to stay away from you?" She said, her anger building up.
"Stay away! You asked Kanhaiya to stay away from us, how could you, Yashoda?"
"Yashoda, Krishna does not just belong to you, he is ours too, how can you stop him from coming to our house?" the Gopis burst.
"You are taking it wrongly, ladies. I just asked him not to steal from you, I didn't ask him not to go to your house or not talk to you," Yashoda explained.

"But Krishna isn't talking to us anymore", they said with disappointment
"If he stops coming to our house, because you asked him to stop stealing, then let it be, you don't have to say anything to him" one Gopi cried out.

"All children are naughty, you don't have to be so harsh on him, Yashoda, if he steals, we can scold him, and you can give him some light punishment, but please don't tell him not to come to our house again," Chandra pleaded
"If you are asking him to stay away from us, you are punishing us, more than him" Jyoti added
Yashoda Maiya was flustered, she was about to say something
but Rohini Devi came in
"Alright, Krishna will come to your house. Go now," she said, smiling
Pleased with her words, they left happily.
"I don't understand ", Yashoda maiya said in confusion
"O Yashoda, such is your lala's Lila, nobody actually understands it, he is even making the Gopis miss his mischiefs," Rohini Devi explained as she smiled

Yashoda maiya also couldn't help but chuckle. She called her son, who was playing with Dau, forgetting all worries in the world.
"Lala, why don't you go play outside, if you meet Chandra or Prabha, say hello to them" maiya insisted
Little Kanhaiya smirked. He understood that the Gopis had already come and talked to Maiyaa .He nodded and went outside.
"Kanhaiya, looks like your plan worked, now Gopis won't come complaining," Dau said

"Even if they do, Dau, Maiya won't get angry at me" Krishna chuckled

THE CRANE

Nandrani was sitting beside ma Rohini, on a jute bed, they chatted while cleaning some grains.
Few Gopis cleaned the courtyard, some sat churning butter.
"Pranam Nandrani" an elderly Gopi came in
Beside the two boys of Yashoda and Rohini came running in.

"What did they do now?" Ma Rohini whispered to Yashoda with a worried look.

Nandrani came closer to the elderly Gopi and addressed her with warm welcome,

"Lilavati, how have you been? It has been a while since we met, say what brought you to Nandbhavan today? Is everything alright? "

"Has the boys troubled you?" She added with a pause as she gave a stern look to her Lalla

"Trouble? No no, o Yashoda, how can your sons ever be a trouble, they are so beautiful, lovely, caring and quiet, they are nicest kids I have ever seen "Lilavati chuckled

Ma Yashoda and Rohini looked at each other they were both pleased and surprised, it was after a long time that a Gopi didn't come complaining to their door.

"Quiet? Of course, ma Yashoda's son is so quiet that he can finish up all the butter in your storehouse without you even realizing that when he came and when he went "a Gopi standing behind ma Yashoda joked.

"If you never know when I come and when I go, how do you even know that it's me? And if you don't know certainly, Why do you come complaining to my mother?" Krishna replied back

Balaram gave a chuckle as the flustered Gopis tried to find words to fight against that argument.

"Leave that be!" Ma Rohini said
"Lilavati you have come after a long time, come inside, we have a lot to catch up"

"Maiya, shall we leave now?" Asked Krishna
"Leave where?" maiya Yashoda asked with concern

"Our friends are waiting for us" Krishna replied

"It is already so late now, what will you do with sun scorching over your head, you need not go today, tell your friends you will come tomorrow" said maiya Yashoda

Krishna and Balaram looked at each other disappointed, they had to go out today, their friends have been waiting for so long but now their mother isn't letting them go.

Krishna quietly went to ma Rohini and sat beside her
"Mother Rohini, my friends won't let me play with them anymore if I break my promise today. They have warned me this is my last chance. Please convince maiya" he said with watery eyes and pouty mouth

"Alright" mother Rohini smiled as she patted his head.

"Yashoda let them go, their sons of cowherd men, they should learn to be stronger, and It is important that they learn to be responsible from this age onwards" Ma Rohini used her words cleverly she knew that mother Yashoda won't deny if it meant that her son will learn good sanskar.

"Alright, but come before it gets dark!"
Krishna and Balaram were finally relieved.
They quickly took their things and ran outside before maiya Yashoda could change her mind.
Soon Krishna met his friends.
"What took you so long?" Subala asked
"We thought we had to wait another yug just for you two", sridama added
"It's not that we won't wait for you if it takes ages" said Madhumangal while munching his snacks
"You couldn't even wait to taste your snacks and are talking big talks about waiting" teased Subala
"Who said I couldn't wait? I was just tasting it for Krishna, mother said to give him the munchiest ones only" Madhumangal said with slight anger
"Alright! Alright!" Balaram laughed at his friends bantering
"Let's go near the river banks" Krishna suggested
"That would be perfect for this scorching afternoon" Sridama said

"We can't be gone for long Kanha, don't you remember mother Yashoda allowed us outside only at one condition, that we arrive before dusk" Balaram said with concern

"Don't worry Dau, we would be back, before she misses us" Krishna said with an assuring smile

"If we had to come back before she starts to miss us, we won't be able to take a second step outside our door" Balaram replied
Krishna only smiled and nodded knowing that Balaram words couldn't be more true.

"Dau, we won't take that long, we would take just a dip and come back" Subala added as his rest of friends supported
Balaram couldn't refuse the pleas of his friends.

The boys brought chaos onto the banks of the peacefully flowing Yamuna, they dived into its waters. The ripples hit the banks, the fishes were surprised by the sudden disturbance.

And soon their fear turned into glee when they realized it's their beloved Krishna who has joined them for a swim.

Our little blue boy, swam along the fishes, they swirled around his body, Alas, the missed fortune of the life on land who missed what the aquatic life witnessed.

The silver fishes swirling around that boy whose body was in the hue of the dark monsoon clouds. He was adorned with bright yellow garments and golden jewelry. The water played with his hair, as his yellow turban loosened The peacock feather still stayed steadily fixed on his turban, unwilling to abandon his Swami, just swaying proudly.

And the fishes kissing his feet and the loose white garlands dangling from his neck. Soon Krishna came to the surface, his friends still splashing and running around. All the heat was forgotten, all of them played merrily in the waters of Yamuna.

But soon a huge shadow floated over their heads, as they looked up they couldn't understand whose shadow fell upon them.
"Is that a cloud?" One of them said.
"It looks like a huge bird" Subala said
It was indeed a bird, a crane to be exact but no usual one.
He was Bakasur, one of the trusted friends of maharaja Kamsa, he had come for the same deed, that Putna, Trinavrat, and Vatsasur were sent for, getting rid of Kans's fated killer.

Krishna and Bakasur locked eyes just once, before Bakasur soared higher.
Krishna looked at Balaram who gave him a concerned look.
Balaram's face grimaced "Krishna watch out!" He screamed with his hands stretched out.
But before Krishna could assess his situation that big bird dived straight towards him with open beaks and engulfed him.
Seeing this horrific scene, Balaram fell on his feet
Some of his friends stared into emptiness, some kept yelling his name, and some simply fainted.
The calves kept calling out for him.
All of them in utter shock.
Bakasur smirked at his victory, which was quiet short lived.
He himself found himself in new found shock, when he felt a burning lump in his throat.

The little boy whom he just swallowed was jumping, punching and kicking in his throat.
And not just that his body radiated such energy that Bakasur felt as if he swallowed the sun a thousand times.
Soon he coughed and the boy jumped out of his beak.
Krishna landed right in front of him, on the shallow water.

Bakasur knew all along but realized just now, this boy was no ordinary boy.
Krishna gestured him with his fingers "come on"
Bakasur pecked fiercely, but Krishna dodged him again and again and again till Bakasur got all frustrated and screeched in anger.
At his final attack, Krishna jumped inside his beak but didn't allow the bird to swallow him.
He gripped his upper beak and pushed the lower ones with his legs.
Bakasur stood there in pain, agony and surprise.
The little boy was ripping his beaks apart with his little legs and hands.
And even after using all his strength Bakasur couldn't even resist him, crushing him was a far-fetched dream.
His eyes grew wider and turned red as he saw his beak split open and blood dropping.
And soon he dropped on earth, lifeless.
Krishna came and stood by near him.
His turban, hair and clothes disheveled, but he, himself, remained unscathed.
A spark of life rose from Bakasur's body.
His soul became part of Krishna's divine body, in other words he attained moksha.

Krishna looked at his friends, he called out to them.
As Balaram woke up he saw Krishna's little feet with a blurry vision.
He got up in hurry, his brother was standing there smiling at him.
"O Krishna, what happened?" he exclaimed.
"I was just playing with our guest Dau! Our uncle really loves me, so he keeps sending new friends to play with me" Krishna smirked

Balaram understood, it was yet another futile attempt of Kans to get rid of Krishna.
"Krishna" all his friends came running to hug their friend
"O Krishna, we thought we lost you" cried Madhumangal
"Don't worry Madhumangal, I will never leave my friends" Krishna assured him.
An assurance that Krishna gives all of us, since time immemorial, that he shall never leave anyone that calls him a friend.
"We should return soon, maiya Yashoda would be waiting for us" Balaram reminded his little brother
Krishna nodded and soon all of them ran again with their calves.
Mother Yashoda was anxiously waiting for her child.
Few more moments and dusk will fall on Vrindavan. Her lala should have arrived by now.

"Look there they come!" One of the mothers spotted the young boys coming.
The calves slowing walking beside Krishna, who himself was immersed in playing his flute.
"O Krishna what took you so long?" Maiya Yashoda hugged her son, all covered with mud and dust.
"We were playing maiya" Krishna hugged her back.
His little arms around his maiya and maiya forgot all her worries.

"Maiya Krishna fought with a big crane" the boys boasted as their mothers took them home.
The mothers delightfully enjoyed listening to the Lilas of their beloved boy, just like we do till today.

THE PRIEST

"Flowers have been arranged, the sweets are almost ready, now we just need to wait for Mata Chandra and Prabha to find us a priest for the puja" Lalita Sakhi said as she took out the fresh rasgullas from the hot syrup and filled them in earthen pots.

Radharani and her friends were preparing for the monthly worship ritual for sun God.

They had arranged everything that would be offered but they still had to wait for a priest to arrive.

"I hope they find one this time" Vishakha Sakhi said with dismay in her eyes.
"They will" radharani assured them

"Let's finish our work first and then we can go help them" radharani added

They quickly went back to their work of preparing the sweets for offering.

Meanwhile, Chandra and Prabha were searching everywhere for a priest.
They wanted a knowledgeable priest who would agree to do the ritual for the little Gopis.

As they were walking besides the meadows few sneaky eyes were following them.

"Do you really think we should do this?"
"Yes, I am sure, just follow me"
"But-"

"What but, don't you want those sweets they have prepared, this is the best way to get all of those sweets"

"What if we get caught and what if sun god gets angry at us for pretending to be priests"

"Oh Madhumangal, my dear friend, we won't get caught, the Gopis would be too busy in the ritual to notice anything, they would keep their eyes closed for most of the time and sun God won't get angry at us, we will be worshipping him, he would be pleased by us, and why are you worrying, you are not an imposter, you are a son of a Brahmin family" Krishna said reassuring his nervous friend.

They both were hiding behind the bushes dressed up as priests, as Krishna had planned to pretend to be a priest to enter the sun temple, the excuse and the bribe he gave Madhumangal were the sweets that were going to be offered but the real reason he took all the pain of dressing up and mugging up the mantras was just to get a good glimpse and sit near radharani.

He had heard that the last time the Gopis arranged for this puja, all month but couldn't find a priest for performing the ritual.

This time he was breaking several pots with one stone, Madhumangal would get his sweets, radharani and her friends would get a priest and our dear lord Krishna would get to sit beside the queen of Vrindavan and take a good glance at her.

All the creatures at Vrindavan long for one glance of Krishna. His beauty has captured the hearts of all the residents, humans and animals all alike.

But Krishna's heart, it was long taken by that beautiful braj Gopi who resided in the palace of Vrishbhan Maharaj, she was the Daughter of the chief of Barsana.

Her beauty was beyond this world, her complexion golden as sun, her hair locks black as midnight, her eyes as of the doe, Her grace and elegance as of a swan, her voice as sweet as jaggery, her one smile pierced and captured his heart.

Just like we couldn't understand how Krishna captivated us, Krishna fails to understand radharani and her enchantment. That's is why they call her Madanmohanmohini, she entranced the person that enchants even the cupid.

Just like Gopis of Vrindavan found different excuses to see Krishna, Krishna searched for different excuses and made various plans just to see his beloved radharani.

And today's mission was one of them.
He had done a lot of practice to pose as the perfect priest and now all they had to do was not get caught.

"Now" Krishna gestured Madhumangal, it was cue to take positions according to Krishna's plan

They soon started walking in front of the Gopis who were disappointed in their search.

"Chandrika, it will be noon soon, we haven't yet found a good priest for the ceremony" sighed Prabha

"O dear Hari, now only you can show us some way, help us to find a priest for our little Gopis ceremony"
Chandrika prayed

"Look!" Prabhavati quickly grasped her arm to get her attention.
Her eyes caught the two priests walking in front of her.
Their gait suggested they were some revered priests who posed grace even when walking in the scorching daylight.

The Gopis didn't want to miss this opportunity, the lord has heard us, that's what they thought, and they weren't wrong, Hari indeed answered their prayers, he himself was posing to be their priest and his plan had just begun.

"O revered one, please stop!" Chandra cried as she hurried to catch up with them

The two priests stopped and turned around.
Their body wrapped in orange robes, their head covered with orange turban and the plain white turban ornaments dangled over their small faces, enough to help them not get recognized.

"O dear priests, may we ask your names and where are you from?"
They politely asked the priests

"I am Pandit Vishnuprasad, this is Madhuprasad we are from Acharaya Garg's ashram in Mathura, we were just returning after completing a ceremony"

"O dear priest , this is such a good news , we were finding someone proper to complete the worship ritual for our little girls, but couldn't find anyone until now, it is indeed lord Hari's mercy that we found you on your way back" Chandrika said with a gleaming smile

"What kind of ceremony are we talking about, I apologize, we only worship the sun god" said Krishna, who was posing to be a Pandit said

"That's such a joyful news, we seek someone for worshipping the sun God himself", said Prabhavati, finally in relief to find someone perfect for the role.

"O revered ones please bless us with your presence and complete the ritual for us" both of them pleaded

"Very well! But you must do the preparations religiously and in time, I cannot bear to offend my lord" said the revered priest

"O dear priest you shall not worry about that, all the preparations are done beforehand, we were only in wait of someone who can complete the rituals, we can go to the Suryakund Mandir even now if you like" said Chandra with satisfaction

"What about the sweet offerings?" said his accomplice, Krishna gave a side eye to Madhumangal

"Yes, yes they are ready too, we have prepared different kind of sweets to please the lord, rasgulla, Sandesh, ladoo, jalebi, rasmalai, everything has been prepared by our girls, they have worked meticulously for many days, o revered ones kindly accompany us and complete the ritual before the auspicious time is gone"

The revered priests nodded, satisfied with the answers.

"Lead the way" said the chief priest, as if he doesn't know each and every path of Vrindavan.

They soon reached the place, the three little Gopis were already waiting there, with baskets filled with flowers, garlands and pots filled with sweets.

They had just finished their work when they received the message from a Gopi who met Chandra and Prabha on the way.

She told them to wait at the Mandir with the offerings till the older ladies find a priest. They were anxiously waiting for them to come with a priest.

When they saw the two elder Gopis arriving and the priests walking behind them, their joy knew no bounds and now they finally could complete the ritual without any worry.

"Radha, Lalita, Vishakha, meet the priests, they are the disciples of Acharya Garg and have come from Mathura, offer your obeisance to them and thank them for accepting our invitation, said Prabhavati.

The Gopis folded their hands and paid their respects to the revered priest.

As they bowed their heads, Radha noticed something.
The feet of the chief priest resembled the lotus feet of Krishna. Soft and gentle, adorned with a flower anklet.

The priests sat on the planks and prepared the sacred fire.

"Please take your seats" the chief priest asked the ladies

They took their seats a bit farther from the priests so as not to offend the celibates.

"Please keep the sweets near to us" said Pandit Madhuprasad

Inviting another side eye from his accomplice.

"It will be easier to make the offerings", he explained.

The Gopis arranged the sweets, and soon the priests began with the rituals.

They chanted the mantras with utmost sincerity, did the ritual without any mistakes, their beautiful mudras and enchanting mantras tranced the Gopis.

"I have never heard such beautiful enunciations of mantras before," said Chandrika

"I have never met such revered priests before," said Prabha
Pleased with the priests that they found they praised the priests and their own good fortune.

While the other Gopis kept their eyes closed and meditated the mantras, Radha slowly opened her eye to take a peek at the priest.

She looked at him from head to toe, left and right, noticing every detail, including his voice and posture.

"Radha, you are a pious lady and that man is a celibate, don't look at him like that", Lalita Sakhi joked. She had caught Radha looking at the priest for a long

"I am not looking at him with those intentions", she shrugged
Both of her Sakhis gave her a curious yet mischievous look
"Look at him, doesn't he seems familiar" said radharani pointing out to the chief priest

"Really? Whom? "Vishakha Sakhi asked
With feigned curiosity
"Krishna" Lalita Sakhi suggested

"Yes" radharani said strongly

"I knew it" Vishakha Sakhi nodded
Radharani came at ease that her Sakhis agreed
"You always see him everywhere and in everyone, of course it's him that you see in this priest too," Vishakha Sakhi added
"No, Sakhi it's not like that" radharani tried to convince her Sakhi that it was really him and not her imagination.

"Radha you keep thinking about him all the time, you see Krishna in everyone, and in everything, you hear his flute in the singing of birds, you seek him in Yamuna's dark water, you see him in the dark clouds, you feel him in the passing breeze, it wouldn't surprise me, if you think that this priest is him too" giggled Lalita Sakhi

Radharani was flustered, she had to convince her sakhis somehow "I agree with you, that bewitcher has enchanted me such, that I see him wherever I go, there is no corner where I don't see him, no moment when I don't feel his separation, not a single second where I don't yearn to see him or seek him, it is true that each passing breeze feels like his touch, each bird singing reminds me of his flute notes, but o Sakhi don't blame me, I am not the only one who suffers from this, don't you share the same fate, don't you see him everywhere too"

Her sakhis looked at each other, "of course we do, that bewitcher stays on our mind all the time"

"No matter how hard we try, he doesn't gets off our mind"
"But there is no denial that if we are plagued with his love, your condition is far worse"

"Even now you are seeing him in this priest"
The sakhis argued

"I am not seeing him in the priest, he is the priest" radharani protested

"Look carefully , look at him! , look at his feet ,look at the flower anklet , what priest wear flower anklets, look at his hand , look at his finger ring , doesn't it looks like the one Krishna wears everyday,"

"Look at his companion, doesn't he look like Madhumangal" radharani stated

The Gopis quickly realized the truth in her words, she was right, she wasn't seeing him in the priest, she saw through the priest"

They soon understood that it was the darling of Vrindavan posing as the priest.

Yet they didn't expose him, they quietly sat during the ceremony,

Radharani took few peeks at the priest engrossed in the ritual, while the other Gopis kept their eyes closed for the ritual, And when she closed her eyes, our darling priest took quick glances at her.

When the ritual was done, the elder Gopis offered some pearls as dakshina to the priests but they refused
"O Gopi, we do not need your pearls, our sole satisfaction lies within pleasing our lord, if sun God is pleased that is our dakshina"

"O revered one, please accept them, unless one pays the dakshina, the ritual is considered incomplete", said the Gopis

"If you insist we can accept the sweets that were offered", said Pandit Madhuprasad.

This time, he received approving nods from his accomplice.

"Radha, Lalita, and Vishakha hand the sweets to the priests", Chandrikaa said

Lalita and Vishakha Sakhi each picked the pots filled with Sandesh and ladoos and handed them to Pandit Madhuprasad, whose eyes were eagerly stuck on the sweets.

Radharani picked up the pot filled with rasgullas and went to Pandit Vishnuprasad, she tilted her head to take a better peek at the face covered by the dangling ornaments of the turban.

But Pandit quickly bowed his head to prevent any mishap. Radharani gave a slight smirk and handed him the pot. Their eyes met for a brief moment.

"O dear priests, we are grateful that you accepted our invitation today, kindly bestow us with your presence even the next month" Prabha said

"Sure" Pandit Madhuprasad accepted the invitation eagerly "We shall take your leave now" said Pandit Vishnuprasad

As they left, the elder Gopis kept praising their poise, their pronunciation and how modest they were to accept sweets instead of pearls.

"Mata Chandra, Mata Prabha, We shall take your leave now" said Radha to the elder Gopis as she hurried, her sakhis followed her.

"Where are we going?" Asked Vishakha as she tried to catch up with her sakhis pace

"To take darshans of our revered priests," Lalita Sakhi joked

They giggled.

Soon they reached, where Krishna and Madhumangal were removing their disguise, finally able to rest, "Look, Krishna we have got so many of sweets, the aroma itself is making me hungry" Madhumangal rejoiced over their success

Krishna noticed someone standing behind the trees, taking a peek at them, upon looking for a while he understood it was none other than radharani and her sakhis, to avoid being questioned and get caught by them he quickly grabbed Madhumangal.

"Let's go back to our cows, Dau must be searching for us" he said as he quickly pulled Madhumangal away.

As he took him away he quickly looked back, radharani was standing beside a tree giving him a smirk.

He understood he had been caught and yet the Gopis were letting him go.
Soon they reached where their friends were
"Where were you?" Dau asked

"Doing a pious job," Krishna replied

Madhumangal explained to Dau everything that happened and went ahead to share the sweets with everyone

"Didn't Radha see through you?" Dau gave Krishna a smirk

"She did" Krishna smiled
"And she just let you go?" Dau was surprised
Krishna just nodded" she hasn't punished me"
"Yet" he added
Krishna sat smiling, he picked up a rasgulla and put one in his mouth, as he relished the sweetness knowing, that when radharani will punish him, to him, it will be sweeter than this.

THE CAVE

It was another day in the kingdom of Nandmaharaj,
As the sun rose, Gopis began their chores of the day. Elders of the houses did their daily routine and went about on their business. Some went to the market, some took their cows to grass lands.

The kitchen bustled with the tinkling of the utensils, noises of the earthen pots clanking, the crackles of firewood, the anklets of the Gopis tingling and their bangles clashed; all these fine sounds could be heard in the quiet dawn.

Although the quiet didn’t stay for long, it was broken as soon as the kids woke up. Their mother hurriedly got them bathed and dressed as they just couldn’t wait anymore to continue their play, with their beloved Kanha, the son of Nandmaharaj.

As soon as they received their mother’s approval, they rushed to Nandbhavan.

Nandrani saw the little Gopals running towards her house.
“Nandrani call Kanha!” Subala said while catching his breath, “Kanhaiya, hurry up!” others yelled.

“Calm down, little ones, your friend won't be coming any sooner. Your dear king is still asleep and won't listen to his mother calling” Nandrani replied

The little boys were disappointed and weren’t ready to give up or wait more. Right after ma Yashoda went back inside, they began with their shoutings “Krishna, hurry up, we need to resume our play”

When that didn't seem to work, they shouted, "Krishna, show some responsibility, your cows are waiting for you"
"Krishna, don't you want to play with us?"
They were using all tactics to bring their friend out.
Here, his friends were screaming their lungs out, there our little blue boy was sleeping blissfully in his room.

Our darling boy opened his eyes when mother Yashoda came again to remind him that this was the last time she was waking him up gently.

He got up and stretched his little hands above his head, he yawned and smudged his mascara as he rubbed his eyes.
He quickly reached the window; the bright morning inspired him to embark towards the unexplored parts of the forest.

"Your friends have been waiting for so long, you'd better hurry up or else they will leave without you" Hearing his maiya's words, Krishna anxiously asked his mother to get him ready hurriedly.

After bathing and dressing him in yellow garments, she adorned him with a pearl necklace and a turban decorated with flowers and dangling pearls.

He didn't wait a moment after being dressed. He rushed to his friends.

"There you are!"
"We thought we would have to wait another yug for you"
Krishna smiled, "Won't you wait for me?"
He teased his Sakhas, knowing very well they would never be tired of waiting on him.

"Stop with your talks, we should hurry, our cows would be waiting for us", Sridama interrupted the chatter

Here, as the Gwalas squabbled, there the cows, were waiting to see their beloved Govinda.

"Maiya, when would Krishna come?" said little Vamsi Priya, a little calf who was part of the herd that Krishna reared.
"As soon as he wakes up, my dear" her mother replied.
"I don't want to wait any more", little Vamshipriya sighed.
And she didn't have to wait anymore, soon they saw the boys rushing in.

As soon as they entered the shed, Krishna caressed his calves and Vamshi along with others started jumping and licking him, "Friends! I have an idea, why don't we go to the unexplored parts of the forest, our mothers have given us a lot of food for today, we can share and have a picnic, we can also play new games while we are there"

Hearing this the boys yelled "yes" in unison.

They quickly took their herd and followed Krishna.
Krishna's flute could be heard by all the creatures of the forest as he walked down the trails of the forest with his cows and his friends.

His curls gently swayed with the breeze, his earrings dangled. The majestic peacock feather dancing, fixed to his turban, as if sitting on a golden throne.

The garland around his neck made with white jasmine flowers dangled loosely as he moved gracefully step by step.

The trees dropped theirs flowers on him as offering, birds moved to lower branches to get a closer glimpse of him. The boys ran and jumped in glee, and the calves ran after them.

Vamshipriya was running a little behind Krishna. She wanted to be closer to him, so she galloped and hurried her pace. Soon she reached him and licked his foot.

Krishna giggled, "Oh, Vamshi, that's so ticklish"
He placed his flute in the rope that was tightly secured at his waist,
He sat down and embraced Vamsipriya with both of his hands.
Vamshipriya was waiting since dawn for this moment. She licked his face and rejoiced his embrace.

Soon all the calves near Krishna wanted to be in his embrace, they rushed to him and started licking him to get his attention, gently budging him with their heads.

Seeing Krishna under this friendly ambush, his friends couldn't stop laughing.
"Stop laughing and help me" Krishna's voice could be heard from under those pearl white calves.
Soon, the peacock feather could be seen along with his little hand waving and asking for their help.
They laughed and laughed till they hurt their tummies, then satisfied to their heart's content, they finally decided to help their poor friend, from the ambush.
They moved the unwilling calves to the side and pulled their friend.
"Phew, took you some time", Krishna said as his friends unapologetically chuckled

Soon, Krishna and his friends were back on their journey. Throughout the trails, they laughed and enjoyed all kinds of games; they didn't stop having fun even for a moment. Finally, after being exhausted, they decided to halt for a while to rest.

Krishna sat with his calves slowly caressing their heads, while some of his friends got bored after a moment of rest, so they decided to play ball.

Madhumangal and Subala were quarrelling about who was better at the game, just then the ball rolled to the other side.
"Don't keep standing, go pick it up" Subala said
"You always make me fetch the ball" Madhumangal sighed as he went to pick up the ball.
Just as he lifted the ball, his eyes caught the most majestic cave he had ever seen.

It had a large entry and on top of it grew large trees and it was covered with creepers and climbers,
"Look!" he yelled, trying to get the attention of all his friends.
They soon gathered near the edge of the cliff, and down below stood the majestic cave.
"It is so big" Gopal said
"And so long" another boy added
"And so scary" Madhumangal added
"Let's go there" two of the boys shouted
"Krishna! Let's go and explore this cave," they looked at Krishna with pleading eyes
"You all may go!" Krishna said with a soft smile
"You won't come with us?" asked Subala
"One of us should stay here with our calves. I will stay, you all can go," Krishna replied.
They agreed and ran towards the majestic cave.

Upon reaching the cave's entrance, they stood awestruck.

"Look at it, doesn't it resembles like a large snake?" Subala said
"Yes, one who has kept its mouth open just to eat us" Madhumangal showed his concerns
"It can't eat us" Sridhama reassured him
"Yes, it's not an actual snake, it just looks like one" Subala added.
"Look carefully, look at the long road that we ran on it resembles its tongue and those rock coming down the roof look like fangs" Vrisabh said
"And the rotten smell must be his breath" Madhumangal added covering his nose.
"It is so dark, inside, why don't we go and explore it" Subala beamed with excitement
"Yes" everyone except Madhumangal said in unison.
"I don't think it is a good idea," Madhumangal said in hesitation

"What are you so afraid of? We are not kids anymore, brave men don't get afraid of such small things, we will be able to protect ourselves" Subala tried convincing him

"Madhumangal, don't be afraid, this is not a real snake, even if it was, it will never be able to swallow all of us together. Even if he does, he won't able to swallow Krishna, Krishna will kill him and protect us just like he killed Bakasur" Sridhama reassured Madhumangal.

Hearing Krishna's name, Madhumangal could finally breathe.
He looked back, he saw Krishna sitting farway on the cliff, playing his flute.

As Madhumangal watched his friend enjoying his time with the calves, Aghasur was watching his plan unfold successfully.

Oblivious to all this happening, the calves were playing around Krishna.
Krishna paused for a while as he realised that his friends had gone for a long time, he stood up to take a look at how far they had gone.

He saw his friends entering the great cave. He was worried that they might get late, but soon his worry shifted to a different reason,
He noticed the cave breathing, he took no time to recognise that this wasn't a cave but the demon Aghasur disguised as a cave.
He didn't wait another second, he rushed towards the "cave" that was waiting for him since the morning.

As he stepped inside his mouth, Aghasur was beaming with pride, for his plan was coming to fruition, but little did he know that the one who entered his mouth was not his victim but his death bearer.

After few steps ahead Krishna, found his friends laying in the venom pool.
For a moment grief engulfed him, but he had no time to pause, Aghasur had already begun with the next phase of his plan.

He twisted his own body, to crush the boys inside.
Krishna resisted and pushed his hands against the walls of his gut and began growing in size. Aghasur was no ordinary demon himself as Krishna became big, he became bigger.

The demigods were astonished to see this scene, they couldn't understand the situation.

Aghasur was getting big and bigger, every tree around him getting crushed.

He kept getting bigger until he could grow no more Unfortunate for him his Maya, his powers were limited but Krishna's weren't.

He did not know the little boy who fearlessly ran inside him was the almighty himself. Even when he no longer could grow more, Krishna could and he did.

Aghasur began choking, soon his skull punctured as his last breath escaped out and he lost his life. After he collapsed, Krishna woke his friends up gently, and walked outside.

That majestic cave now looked more like a snake's carcass. When they reached outside, all the cowherd boys rejoiced and celebrated their savior. Krishna quietly sneaked away from the celebration, he went near the fallen demon's body, Aghasur's soul was still waiting there, as Krishna approached, the soul entered Krishna and became one with him.

THE PICNIC

"I can hear my tummy grumbling," said Madhumangal
"It is good then, that we have a lot of food packed with us" Krishna giggled

"Look around, doesn't this looks the perfect picnic spot, our cows are happily grazing

And the weather is also so pleasant, why don't we sit down and have our picnic here" Krishna said

All the Gwalas sat around Krishna, they took out their packed food and presented it to Krishna, one said "Krishna look I have sweet rasgullas, my mother freshly prepared them this morning"
Other one said "look I have crispy Kachoris filled with spicy filling"
"Oh Krishna, I have your favorite butter" another friend said
"My mother sent Aam Ras for all us" Subala said
Krishna's Plate was filled with a little food from all his friends, the leaf platter in his hand was full of delicacies, rasgullas, Kachoris, Aam Ras, jalebis, kheer and Makhan dripping down his hand to his elbows.

While Krishna and his friends were enjoying the picnic on bhulok, the inhabitants of Jaya Lok were celebrating his victory over the snake demon Aghasur. Aghasur was a demon that terrified even the, mighty inhabitants of heaven
When they found that the little boy of Vrindavan has defeated the demon they were assured.

That the little cowherd boy was no other than their almighty lord Vishnu.

Their praises and chants reached the ears of brahma dev who was meditating in his Brahmalok disturbed by the noise he asked his disciple what was happening, his disciple gave him a brief of how the little cowherd boy had defeated a demon that even heaven was terrified of, upon hearing how the inhabitants of Jaya Lok were convinced that the little kid was their almighty Vishnu brahma couldn't help but scoff
"They believe a kid could be Vishnu" brahma couldn't understand their confusion.

What has the kid achieved to be compared to my almighty lord, he thought to himself

"I want to see the kid myself" he declared
He sat on his swan, and went to see the little cowherd boy himself.

When he reached there he saw the view that was cherished by the birds of Vrindavan every day, He saw the kids sitting as a lotus formation, at the centre sat a little boy, with dark bluish complexion he wore yellow garments and a turban decorated by flowers and peacock feathers. He was eating the half-eaten food of his friends, spilling as he ate, with curry on his face, dripping from his little fingers, over his clothes.

He saw this scene and was dumbfounded, how this little kid was being compared to his lord Vishnu.

"This kid!" He exclaimed
"Has the heavenly beings lost their mind, how can they compare a village boy to my lord" he asked his disciples
"It's true, my lord, this little kid is so small, yet has performed so many miracles already, no doubt the heavenly beings believe him to be an avatar of lord Vishnu"

Brahmadev wasn't convinced at all, "what are these miracles, you are talking about?"

"Brahmadev, when this boy was just a few days old baby he killed demoness Putana, after not long after he defeated the storm demon Trinavrat, and now look at that empty carcass of Aghasur, the demon whom even heaven feared was trounced by this child as if he was playing some game"

Brahma still wasn't convinced, "I don't believe this boy to be Vishnu, you want me to believe that my lord Vishnu took Avtaar and I was unaware of it, I am the creator of this universe, nothing happens here without my knowledge"

"If you still insist then I can take a little test of this imposter" he declared

His disciple hesitated, "you will test Vishnu" this thought seemed unsettling to him.

Brahmadev remained adamant, "well if he really is Vishnu my little test would be no big deal to him" he said

"What is your plan?" His disciple asked

Brahmadev gave a sly look he looked at the boys merrily chatting and feasting and then looked over to the calves happily grazing in a little distance , he went to the calves first. His plan was to kidnap the calves first and when Krishna would go looking for them he would kidnap the rest of the cowherd boys.

Just as he planned he vanished the calves first then the little boys. When Krishna couldn't find any of his dear friends or calves, he thought to himself that what was happening, it was unlike of his friends to just disappear like that and even if the calves went astray they couldn't have gone so far away that none of them could be seen.

"First Vamsipriya, Laxmi and other calves went missing and now Subala, Madhumangal and other boys are nowhere to be seen either, I just left them eating a minute ago, where could they have gone and they even left the food as it is."

Krishna thought
It didn't take too long for him to realize what was happening, first Aghasur tried to trick him and now brahma was testing him, he surely was having an eventful day.

"I could play along with brahma as much as he wants, if he wants to test me so be it, I am prepared for all his tests but I can't let my beloved mothers suffer for the sake of his tests, I will have to come up with a solution before I go home"
He thought and thought and then finally smiled back at the sky.

He was determined to not let the mothers know that their sons have gone missing, he decided to take the forms of his friends and calves and take their places till brahma brings back the original boys and calves.

"Dear mothers I shall now fulfill your deep desire of having me as your own child" he said as he expanded himself into all the cowherd boys and calves.

When Krishna returned that evening, the mothers were already waiting by the village entry as the sun had long set

and it was dark already, when Krishna returned with his friends, the mothers rushed to welcome them.
They noticed their sons were glowing more vibrantly, their aura was as charming and divine as Nandmaharani's son.

Many months went by like that.

The mothers enjoyed Krishna's presence as their own son, They bathed him , clothed him, decorated him as they liked, they made so many dishes and fed him with their own hands, to everybody else seeing outside , it seemed they were caring for their own child but suddenly they had become even more fond of them,

Not just mothers even the fathers were taking care of their sons gently, they wouldn't scold them for their mistakes anymore.

Mothers didn't want to send their sons for tending cows and cows refused to let go their calves for grazing, some cowherd men even complained how the cows would push them or kick them if they tried to take their calves whom they wouldn't stop licking and embracing.

One afternoon when the kids were preparing to leave for the meadows, the mothers stopped them as they have been doing for the past few months, before that the mothers eagerly sent them off to be able to complete their chores undisturbed

Balaram had noticed all the odd behavior of the villagers, the children carried a powerful aura like his little brother.

Not just that the parents have become more soft and lenient to their children.

When they finally reach the meadows, some cows that were grazing nearby noticed the little calves and came running downhill, the cows licked the little calves as the little ones sucked the milk out of their teats.

The men tending to them came running after them, they were visibly upset that they had to follow the cows all the way, but their anger subsided as soon as they caught a glimpse of their children.

They took them into their arms and patted their heads, talked to them lovingly, they forgot about the reason they had to run downhill altogether, Balaram looked at the men and then looked back at the calves who were still caressing their calves.

He took a better look at them and realized, the cows who were not mother to these calves were also feeding their milk to them.

And then he looked at his little brother standing a far, smiling at the scene. Balaram went to him, crossed his arms and questioned his relaxed brother, who didn't seem confused about the current situation like Balaram.

"Krishna, what is happening over here?"
"What Dau? Ahh you mean the parents being so loving to their OWN children" Krishna smiled with feigned innocence
"Isn't it how it supposed to be" he added

Balaram gave him a stern look, he knew his tricks very well, and his feigned innocence, that was a skill he witnesses everyday, whenever some Gopi comes running to complain to their mothers.

"You want to tell me something?" Balaram raised an eyebrow
Krishna just nodded still keeping up with his act.
Done with his games, Balaram asked directly," Are all these calves and cowherd boys, you?" although this was a rhetorical question, Balaram already knew that those calves and boys who have enchanted the whole village can be none other than Krishna himself.

Krishna finally gave in, and nodded his head in yes
"But why? Where are our friends?" Balaram wasn't present there the day Krishna killed Aghasur and brahma kidnapped his friends, unaware with everything that was going on.
Krishna finally explained everything to him, how brahma stole the calves and the boys and how Krishna has been filling in for them for a whole year.

"But for how long will you play along with brahma's scheme?" Dau asked
"Not much more, the time has come to show brahma, his mistake"
Krishna replied as he kept his hand on Balaram's shoulder, reassuring him.
The brothers resumed their day as if nothing had changed, Krishna was playing with his
'Friends', while the cow happily grazed nearby.
Meanwhile, in brahma Lok brahma was curious to know that what did the little imposter did after losing all his friends and calves.

He returned to earth to have a look,
When he reached there, he saw Krishna playing with his friends while the calves grazed nearby
Confusion, he hit him, didn't he take these very boys and calves to his Brahma Lok,
How can they be present here? Who were these people?
Krishna took a glance at the flustered Brahma. He rested his palms on his waist and smirked, Soon all the boys and calves took the form of Krishna, then all the Krishna's took the form of four -armed Vishnu, with the golden crown on his head and his divine Sudarshan chakra, lotus,
conch shell and club in his four hands.

As Krishna stood at the centre while all the Vishnus surrounded him,
Brahma, as he witnessed the scene, was too dumbfounded to speak, he realised his mistake,
He couldn't understand how he did not recognise his own lord; he now understood his grave mistake,
He came down and bowed his head in front of the little cowherd boy who was indeed his own
Lord Vishnu.

"O god! How did I commit such a grave mistake, how could I not recognise you?" Brahma
exclaimed in dismay
"O brahma, you were too indulged in your pride for your knowledge, you in your false ego Forgot that you are not the original creator of the universe, you forgot that you yourself were created by me, then how could you recognise the one you forgot?" Krishna said in a calming voice, no anger, no offence, just as a parent guides their children.

"Oh, Brahma, you wanted to test me, so now tell me, did I pass your test? Do you now believe that I am indeed Vishnu, your beloved lord" Krishna added
"O Krishna! O my dear lord, forgive me as I forgot that your divinity cannot be tested, it does not seek or submit to proof, it can only be revealed by faith,
I got engrossed in my false ego and got blinded by your Maya, I forgot you, forgive me

Krishna, you are the supreme the lord, this whole world has come from you, you are the origin and the multi-universe and the planets are like pearls, and you are the string that holds it" Krishna smiled, Brahma knelt down near his lotus feet, bowing his head and pleading for his
forgiveness.

"O brahma, how can I be angry at you? You are my beloved devotee, after all I came on this earth on your request, I just wanted to pull you out of your ignorance, to remind you that you are not the only brahma, apart from this universe, there are many universes, each having their own Brahma, who has many more heads and much more power and knowledge than You, You, and all of them came from me, and that I am your and the entire creation's origin" Krishna replied to his pleas.

"Dear lord, I am grateful for your mercy, but one thing still perplexes me, how is that these cowherd boys don't notice your greatness how is that even after your mighty feats they still see a little boy in you" brahma asked in confusion, he agreed that in his ignorance he believed that lord Vishnu couldn't be on earth without him knowing, but why these kids couldn't see that their friend was not an ordinary child, how were they so at ease, in roaming around him, playing with him, and even teasing him.

"O brahma, these cowherd boys and girls of Vrindavan see me as their own, what covers their eyes is not ignorance but love, they truly see me beyond the veil of Maya"
Krishna answered his query
"They love me hence they don't bother if I am great or insignificant, if I am killing strong demons or if I am hiding behind my mother, they see only me, Krishna, the boy they love, Oh, Brahma, for only the ones who love me can see me; no penance, no knowledge is enough to get me, but the ones who love me even in the smallest bits, for them I am easily attainable, their love binds me, then I belong to them, in whatever form they might want me as"
"Brahma if you leave your false ego behind, and love me, pour your heart into pure devotion,
You too will be able to see the real me and attain me"

Krishna gave him an answer that finally put his heart at ease, "o my dear lord, I now understand the greatness of the residents of Vrindavan, dear lord, I ask you of only one favour that in my next life I don't want to be any higher celestial being, I simply want to be a blade of grass in Vrindavan so that I can touch the dust of the feet of your devotees and gain your pure devotion, that is my only request" saying this lord brahma took his lord's blessing and departed from Brahmalok. As he was leaving, Krishna jokingly reminded him to return his friends to him as without them, Vrindavan seems empty to him.

Soon after Brahma left, his friends returned to him along with the calves. When they woke up from their deep slumber all they remembered was their friend leaving to go look for the missing cows, “I found them, they just went a bit behind the slope” Krishna came running “What took you so long, we almost fell asleep” Subala said

“It feels like I have been sleeping for months” Madhumangal said as a yawn escaped his mouth, “If you sleep right after eating so much. What else will happen, let’s go now, our mothers would be waiting for us” Krishna said with a chuckle.

This way the cowherd boys and the calves finally returned to their home.